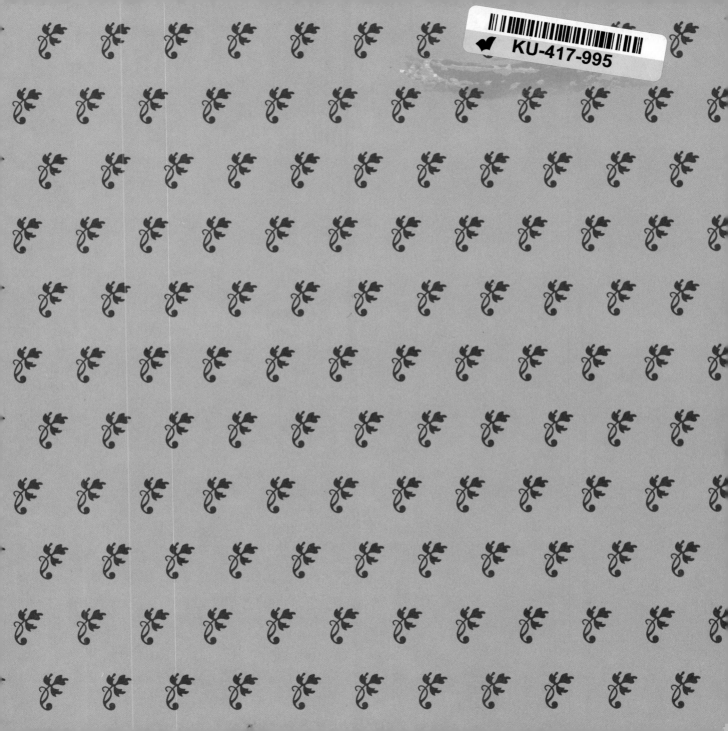

INSTANT

Nailcare

INSTANT
Nailcare
Fabulous nails in next to no time

Sally Norton

Photography: Nick Cole

LORENZ BOOKS

This edition first published in 1998 by Lorenz Books

© Anness Publishing Limited 1998

Lorenz Books is an imprint of
Anness Publishing Limited
Hermes House
88–89 Blackfriars Road
London SE1 8HA

ISBN 1 85967 688 X

A CIP catalogue record for this book is available from the British Library

Publisher: Joanna Lorenz
Senior Editor: Cathy Marriott
Designer: Ian Sandom
Make-up and Hair: Sue Moxley

With thanks to the following companies for the use of products for photography: Mavala,
Elegant Touch, Rimmel, Bourjois, Boots No7, Collection 2000, The Body Shop, Sensiq,
Cutex, Max Factor International, CoverGirl, Freeman's Catalogue, Cacherel.

Printed in Singapore by Star Standard Industries Pte. Ltd.

1 3 5 7 9 10 8 6 4 2

Contents

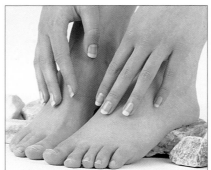

Nailcare

Your hands say a lot about you. They're one of the first things people notice, because they're constantly on view. As well as using our hands for a wide variety of practical tasks, we use them to help express ourselves and to emphasise what we're saying. That's why it's essential to make the most of yours. Everyone can have great-looking hands and you don't have to have long slender fingers and a perfect set of nails to achieve this. Some basic care is all it takes to have soft skin and strong, nicely shaped nails. Once you've achieved this, you can experiment with lots of different looks. This book aims to inform and inspire you.

Above: Red nails always look chic and sophisticated.

Right: Try experimenting with different shades of polish.

Nail Know-how

Beautiful hands and nails have always been in fashion. In the past very long nails were considered ultra-feminine because it showed that you didn't have to work with your hands for a living. In the 1920s, French fashion designer Coco Chanel sported short nails and showed how attractive they could be. Whatever length your nails are, they'll help you look well groomed if you give them a little care and attention. More than that, you can experiment with different looks to match them to your outfit, express your personality or use them as a striking fashion accessory. The only limit is your imagination.

WHAT IS A NAIL?

A nail is mostly made up from keratin, a protein substance that forms the base of all horny tissue, including your hair. It's whitish and translucent in appearance and allows the pinkish colour of the nail bed underneath to be seen. A nail doesn't contain any nerves or blood vessels. The purpose of nails is to protect your fingers, so you can do a wide variety of tasks.

Above: Try a classic red manicure.

Nail bed
The part of the skin the nail rests on. It has many blood vessels that provide the nourishment the nail needs to grow.

Nail root
This is at the base of the nail and is attached to an actively growing tissue known as the matrix.

Free edge
The part of the nail that reaches over the top of the fingertip.

Nail body
The visible portion of the nail that sits on top of the nail bed and extends from the root to the free edge. It is made of lots of thin layers that are held together by oil and moisture to keep it resilient.

Matrix
The part of the nail bed that lies beneath the nail root. It contains nerves, lymph and blood vessels to nourish the nail and produces new cells that create and harden the nail. The matrix will continue to grow as long as it receives nutrition and isn't damaged by injury.

Lunula
The "half moon" located at the base of the nail. The light colour of the lunula is caused by the reflection of light where the matrix and the connective tissue of the nail bed join.

Cuticle
The thin strip of skin around the base of the nail that protects the new cells underneath from infection or damage.

Above: Be as conventional, or as outrageous, as you like when it comes to nail polish colour.

DID YOU KNOW?

■ On average, nails grow about 3 mm (1/4 inch) a month.

■ Nails grow faster in summer time than in the winter.

■ Nails also grow at a faster rate during pregnancy.

■ If you lose a nail owing to an accident, it will take about six months to grow back.

■ Your middle fingernail grows the quickest while the thumbnail grows the slowest.

■ Your toenails grow more slowly than your fingernails.

Right: The natural look can also show off well manicured nails.

The Essential Manicure Kit

If you're serious about having beautiful nails, you need the right tools for the job. While you don't have to have tray upon tray of equipment like they do in beauty salons, you do need these essential items:

Nail files

Emery boards are the best type to choose, and they come in different levels of coarseness. For most people, a medium grade emery board is very useful for shortening nails, and a fine grade one is good for finishing nails and smoothing away any snags. Replace them regularly, as use soon wears away the edges.

Nail buffer

These come in all shapes and sizes. They usually combine three buffing surfaces to smooth away ridges from the surface of your nails and give a wonderful shine. Try to buy a slim one as they're much easier to use.

Manicure scissors

These are useful when you want to trim long nails without spending a long time wielding a nail file. However, always buff any rough edges from your nails after using scissors.

Manicure bath

This is an instant way to bring a touch of the beauty salon into your own nails.

Right: Face up to beautiful nails.

Above: The perfect manicure kit. Clockwise from left: nail file; hoof stick; buffer; polishes; base coat; manicure bath; polish remover; hand cream; treatment oil; manicure scissors; top coat.

Manicure baths are good for holding cleansing ingredients for use on your nails. The top is shaped so you can place your nails into the liquid without spilling it. However, there's no need to buy a specialist manicure bath – any small, shallow bowl will be just as effective.

Hoof stick

These wooden sticks have a rubber tip on the end, shaped like a horse's hoof, to help you push back the cuticles. The other end can be used to gently scrape away any material from beneath the nails.

Cuticle softeners

These soften cuticles, making it easier to push them back. They're also useful for helping to loosen any stubborn skin that's stuck to the nail bed. Cuticle softeners are available in various formulations – from clear liquids you paint on, to thick creams you massage into the cuticle.

Hand cream

This is essential for helping to seal moisture into the skin on your hands. The oils in the formulation also help to strengthen weak nails. Available as lotions and creams – the drier your skin, the richer the formulation you should choose.

Nail treatment oil

Special treatment for weak or fragile nails. Apply it on a daily basis and you'll soon reap the benefits.

Above: Apply base coat to bare nails before coloured polish.

Base coat

This is applied to bare nails and will help create a smooth surface before you apply coloured polish.

Coloured polishes

It's up to you how many you choose, but a wardrobe of colours will allow you to match your manicure to your outfit.

Clear top coat

This is applied over dry nail polish. It lengthens the lifespan of coloured polish because it helps prevent chipping.

Polish remover

This contains solvents to dissolve old nail polish. Look for acetone-free varieties as they're more gentle on your nails.

Left: Build up a wardrobe of polish colours so you can really express yourself!

Right: A simple glass bowl from the kitchen cupboard will double up as a manicure bath.

Hard as Nails!

Weak, flaky nails are the most common manicure complaint. While there's no single magic formula to transform fragile nails into tough talons, there are lots of things you can do to help yourself grow long, strong, beautiful nails. Here are some of the best suggestions.

TOP 10 TIPS TO STRENGTHEN NAILS

1 Always wear rubber gloves when washing up the dishes – soaking nails in water is the number one enemy against nail strength. Also, the detergents will strip away the oils your nails need to be strong. If you find that moisture levels build up in the gloves as your hands perspire, wear a pair of thin cotton gloves underneath to absorb the moisture and protect your nails. Healthier nails are stronger nails.

2 Hand models always wear gloves for household or gardening chores. The chemicals in cleaning materials won't do your hands or nails any good and gardening is sure to leave you with damaged nails.

3 Look for nail polish removers that are acetone-free. This ingredient can leave your nails very dry, which means they're more liable to break. Most good handcare ranges offer them.

4 Don't use your nails as a tool. Even the healthiest, strongest set of nails won't stand up to being used as levers or scrapers. Remember to take a moment to find the right tool for the job rather than risk having to grow your nails from scratch again.

Above: Simple and effective. Pure olive oil will strengthen weak or fragile nails.

5 Soak your bare nails in a bowl of olive oil. Leave them there for 10 minutes, then wipe away the excess with some cotton wool (cotton balls).

6 Most good nailcare ranges offer a nail strengthener lotion to help prevent weak nails from splitting or breaking. Apply it under your base coat.

7 Use the finishing side of a nail buffer to stimulate the circulation of blood in the nail bed.

8 Apply hand cream after each time you wash your hands because it'll help build up oil levels in your nails. Take the time to rub a little into each nail.

9 Once a week, apply a layer of intensive hand cream before bed. Then pull on a pair of white cotton gloves – most good chemists sell them. This will allow the creams to penetrate your hands and nails, and you will wake up to stronger nails.

10 Keep your nails at a sensible short length – they'll be less liable to break.

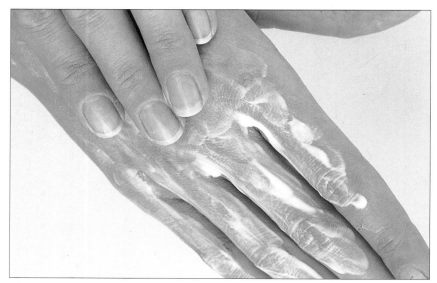

Above: Don't forget the hand cream. It will work wonders on your nails, too.

Right: Toughen up your act for longer, stronger nails.

Eat your Way to Beautiful Nails

The best way to get fabulous nails is by following a healthy, balanced diet. These diet tips will help ensure you're eating your way to longer, stronger nails.

Step up your protein intake

Too little protein can lead to weak nails, so make sure you're getting your fair share. You should eat two portions a day from the following: meat, fish, eggs, cheese or milk.
Try: Pouring semi-skimmed milk over your wholegrain breakfast cereal or having a cheese sandwich on whole-wheat bread for lunch.

Think zinc

Zinc is a mineral needed for the growth and renewal of cells and is important for the formation of new nail cells. Fill up on zinc-rich foods such as whole grains, nuts, seeds, lean meat and seafood.
Try: Snacking on a handful of freshly shelled peanuts or scattering some prawns over a crisp green salad.

Take 5!

You should aim to eat five portions of fresh fruit and vegetables each day to ensure your body is getting all the nutrition it needs.
Try: Having a glass of unsweetened orange juice with your breakfast or bulking out a sandwich with a mixed green salad.

Boost your iron intake

Iron deficiency can make your nails thin and flat, so increase your iron intake through foods such as lean red meat, dark green vegetables, dried fruit and nuts.
Try: Mixing some dried apricots into a container of low fat natural yogurt or steaming some broccoli to have with your evening meal.

Flower power

Flaky dry nails often respond to a supplement of evening primrose or starflower oils because they both contain the polyunsaturated fatty acids needed to form the structure of cell membranes and lock in moisture.

> **Tip**
> Always consult your doctor about any health or diet problems.

Above: Get fruity for beautiful nails.

Right: You are what you eat, where your nails are concerned.

Above: You should aim to eat at least 5 portions of fruit and vegetables per day.

Caring for your Cuticles

Look at any beautiful pair of hands, and you'll see cuticles that are neat and well cared for. Ensuring that your cuticles are well cared for is the cornerstone of any manicure regime.

WHAT IS A CUTICLE?

The thin strip of skin that runs along the base of the nail is called a cuticle. It protects the nail by acting as a barrier against any bacteria that may try to work their way under the nail and damage the live cells that are being formed just underneath.

Cuticle care

It is very important to care for your cuticles properly. If they're neglected and become dry, you could be left with sore, infected nails. If they're pushed back roughly, you run the risk of damaging the new cells underneath. What's more, rough, overgrown cuticles make your hands appear uncared for. A little regular care will ensure that your cuticles are healthy and neat.

CUTICLE TREATMENTS

■ The best time to push back dry or ragged cuticles is right after a bath. You'll get a neater result and find any pieces of skin that adhere to the nail bed easier to remove.

■ Never use clippers on your cuticles. You'll risk leaving your fingers sore and open up your nails to infection. (Many manicurists won't use them for this reason.) Also, using clippers on your cuticles can make them become tougher and thicker than before.

■ There are many cuticle softening creams on the market that help soften the cuticle to make it easier to push back. Modern formulations are fast-acting – that is, you only have to wait a few minutes for results.

■ Nail oils are good news for cuticles. As well as strengthening the nail, they also soften and condition dry cuticles. If you don't have any specialist oil, ordinary olive oil or baby oil will do the trick. Apply it on a daily basis.

1 Apply a little cuticle softener to the cuticle on each nail. Massage it well into the base of the nail with your fingers to ensure that it works properly.

2 Leave it to work for three minutes, or as long as instructed. Then gently push your cuticles back using a hoof stick. If you don't have a hoof stick, use a cottonbud (swab).

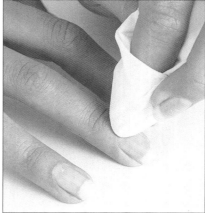

3 Remove any residue with a tissue. Rinse your nails in warm water to ensure that your nails are really clean.

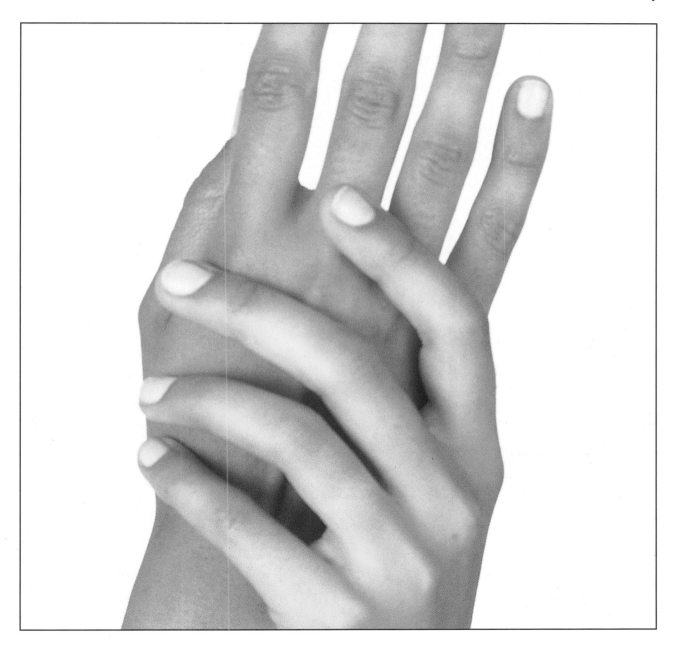

Filing your Nails

It is worth learning the proper filing techniques so you can shape your nails without damaging them.

FILE STYLE

■ While steel nail files may last a lifetime, they're a bad choice because they can tear or split your nails. It's much better to buy a packet of emery boards instead. A general rule to follow is, the weaker your nails are, the finer the emery board you should choose.

■ Have a few nail files on the go at a time. Carry one in your bag or purse at all times, so you can smooth a nail if it snags – rather than having to sacrifice the whole nail tip because it tears.

■ Don't file nails when they're wet because they are more liable to break. If you have extremely weak nails it may be a good idea to file them into shape while you're wearing nail polish for added protection.

■ Never file backwards and then forwards as this can cause the nail layers to split. File in one direction only, using the smooth side of an emery board. Hold the emery board under the nail at a 45 degree angle.

■ Don't file deeply down into the sides of your nails because it exposes the underlying sensitive skin and can lead to infection. It also dramatically weakens your nails.

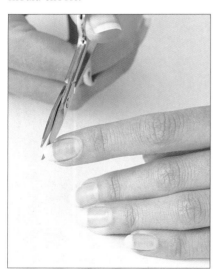

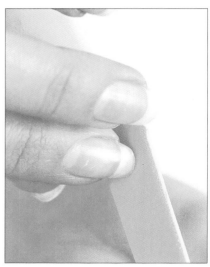

1 If you're making long nails quite a bit shorter, it's quicker and more practical to trim off the excess with a pair of nail scissors. Cut from the side to the middle of the nail, to the length you want. Then repeat on the other side. Don't worry about the final shape at this stage, as you'll correct any defects with the nail file.

2 File each nail from the side to the centre, holding the emery board at a 45 degree angle. This tilting will ensure that you mainly file the underside of the nail. Repeat on all the nails.

3 Hold the file vertically to file just the tip of the nail using a downward motion.

WHAT SHAPE SHOULD I CHOOSE?

Nails vary greatly in shape, but most usually fall into one of four types – square, round, oval and pointed.

■ Nails can be filed in a variety of ways. A slightly squared oval is the most natural looking and flattering shape for all nails. It's also a nail saver because you don't need to file too deeply into the sides of the nails – this is where most breakages start.

■ If you're not sure what shape to file your nails, look at the shape of your nail at the base. The tips of your nails look good when they mirror this shape.

■ Don't wear your nails ridiculously long – it's impractical and old fashioned. Turn your palms facing you. If you can't see any nails extending over your fingertips then your nails are too short. You should see about 1/2cm (1/4 inch) of nail tip for the ideal length.

■ If you work with your hands, a shorter, more rounded shape is usually better in order to avoid nail breakage.

■ If your nails are thin or weak, it's best to keep them fairly short – or they're sure to break. Shorter nails also means stronger nails.

Right: Beautifully shaped nails can easily carry off the brightest and boldest shades of polish.

Pretty Nails, No Polish

Use a nail buffer to create a look that requires low maintenance, is as shiny as clear polish and lasts for up to a week. The only tool you need is a buffer: use the pink side to prime your nails, the white to smooth ridges and the grey to add shine.

The Benefits of Buffing

■ Buffing won't dry out or damage your nails as polish can.

■ It's an excellent way of boosting the circulation of blood in the nail bed, which means healthier, stronger nails in the long term.

■ It will make all nails look better because it smoothes out tiny imperfections in the surface, helping to make them shine.

■ It's a natural look that goes with any make-up look.

■ It's quick and easy, as there is no waiting for polish to dry.

■ It's an easy technique that anyone can master! If you haven't tried many manicure techniques before, it's a good place to start!

Tip
Don't buff until you get a burning sensation at your fingertips – it's a sign you're overdoing it and wearing down the nail.

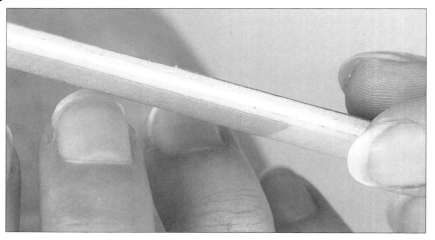

1 Wash your hands with soap and water and dry them well so your nails are free from surface oils. Then, using the rough pink side of the buffer, gently buff backwards and forwards, working from the base of your nails to the tips. This temporarily roughs up the surface of your nails.

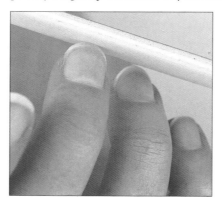

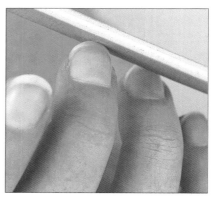

2 Switch to the soft white side of the buffer and buff again. Use a very light pressure and keep going until your nails look nice and shiny.

3 Finish by using the same motion with the smooth grey side until your nails really gleam. A couple of minutes spent at this stage will achieve a shine that lasts for a long time.

Clean, Simple Nails

Everyone loves nails that look healthy and well cared for. Accentuate the tip with a sweep of white nail pencil, then add instant shine with a coat of clear polish. It couldn't be simpler!

ALL WHITE ON THE NIGHT

A white nail pencil is a great manicure tool to keep on hand. Even if you've managed to grow your nails to a respectable length, the tips may not look as even and white as you would like. An instant solution is to apply a little white nail pencil under the free edges of your nails. It lasts until the next time you wash your hands.

■ If you don't have an ordinary clear polish to hand, then a base coat or top coat will work just as well.

■ You can use white eyeliner pencil instead, if you prefer.

■ Sharpen the pencil before using it to make it hygienic to use.

■ If the white pigment clumps under the nail, sweep over it with a clean cotton-bud (swab).

> **Tip**
> Keep the pencil well sharpened to make it easier to apply. If it is quite soft, try storing it in the refrigerator between uses.

1 Apply a coat of clear polish. Allow it to dry thoroughly before applying a second coat. Two thin coats give a better finish than one thick coat.

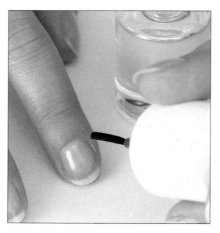

2 Apply a second coat to build up a tough, glassy sheen.

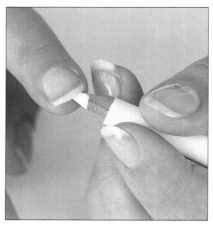

3 Run the white pencil under the free edges of your nails.

The Classic Red Manicure

Red nails always look chic and sophisticated, whether you want to look stylish by day or sexy by night. What you need is a steady hand and a little time to achieve a look that never goes out of fashion.

THE RIGHT RED FOR YOU

Just take a look at the cosmetic counters and you'll discover that there are literally dozens of different reds to choose from. For instance, a soft strawberry red is worlds apart from a striking pillarbox (cherry) shade of red. A good way of deciding which shade of red is right for you is to take a look at the tone of the skin on your fingers – it will suit some shades of red better than others.

■ Pale skin – crimson will create a dramatic contrast against your skin tone.

■ Freckled skin – orange reds will look striking without overpowering your skin.

■ Warm skin – pinky reds will enhance the warm tones of your skin without being too harsh.

■ Olive skin – fiery reds with brown undertones will flatter your skin.

■ Black skin can carry off berry red or burgundy.

Tip
If you have long, elegant fingers, you can carry off dramatic deep reds, russets and burgundies with style.

1 Start with the little finger on your right hand and work inwards, then do the same for your left hand. First apply a coat of clear base coat to prevent the red pigment in your nail polish staining your nails.

2 Apply a stripe of red polish down the centre of your nail.

3 Paint a strip of colour along the side of each nail to finish. The side strokes should meet with and overlap the centre one. Don't overload the brush – one dip into the bottle should do an entire nail. Wait until the colour dries, then apply another coat.

4 Finish with a coat of clear top coat to help guard against chipping.

The 1950s Manicure

In the 1950s, many women wore another version of the classic red manicure. This was basically the same look, except that the half moons at the base of each nail were left clear. This look has come back into fashion recently because it looks so good, but you need a steady hand to apply it.

MANICURE TIPS

■ This is a difficult look to achieve well. If you find the brush is quite unwieldy, pull out a few bristles to make a slimmer brush that's easier to handle.

■ This look suits long slim nails the best. If you have very wide nails, it is best to avoid this look as it'll simply accentuate the breadth of your nails.

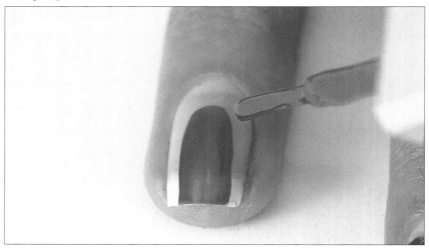

1 Over a clear, protective base coat, apply a stripe of red nail polish down the centre of the nail, starting just above the moon at the base of your nail.

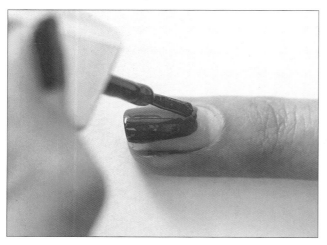

2 Apply a strip of colour to each side of the nail, following the line of the half moon.

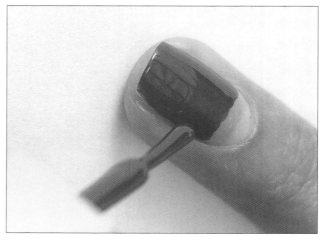

3 Wait until it is completely dry, then apply a second coat of nail polish. Finish with clear top coat, applied over the whole of the nail.

The Perfect Polish for You

There's a vast range of nail polish colours on the market. Experiment to find your favourites, but first take a few factors into account when choosing the most popular nail polish colours.

■ Pale beiges and ivories are a very good choice for short nails because they create a "barely there" finish. They are also a good choice if you don't have much time for manicures, because they don't show up chips quite as much as other colours.

■ Corals, oranges and purples look fabulous against tanned, olive or dark skins. However, avoid them if you have nicotine-stained fingers as they'll just emphasise the problem.

■ Red is a wonderful bold colour on all skin tones and nail lengths. As a general rule, the longer your nail, the brighter the red you can carry off. However, red only looks good on well-cared for hands. There's nothing worse than red, bitten nails!

■ Soft pinks suit everyone's skin tone. Also, they don't require perfect nails to look good.

■ Browns and burgundies work best on young, slim hands. They can emphasize large knuckles or lines.

Below: New nail polish colours are always fun to try – your colour choices are endless.

Above: A soft pink polish will complement most people's skin tone.

The French Manicure

The French manicure is a look that everyone loves because it makes all lengths of nails look clean and healthy. It combines a pink polish over the entire nail with white tips. It's suitable for all occasions, from an ultra-natural to a bridal look. It does take a little practice to get right at first, but it's worth persevering.

Getting the look right

Most ranges of polish include soft pink and white shades that enable you to create the French manicure look. However, it's also worth looking out for special kits that contain everything you need to get the look right. Some kits come complete with pieces of tape that you lay across the nail to allow you to paint on the white polish. However, these tend to leave a ridge of polish when they're removed, which can ruin the look. It's better to draw the white tips freehand. Use a small paintbrush if you find that the brush supplied is too unwieldy.

The American manicure

Another lovely, but less well known manicure look is the American manicure. It's similar to the French manicure, except that you replace the pink base polish with a creamy buff or beige shade. You may find that it's more flattering to your skin tone than the pink polish.

Tip

The key to this look is to wait for each coat to dry thoroughly before applying the next – otherwise, you're sure to end up with smudges.

1 Apply a clear base coat to protect your nails and help to prevent chipping.

2 Apply two thin coats of white polish to the tips of your nails. Try to apply it in one long stroke, working from one side of your nail to the other.

3 Allow the white polish to completely dry, then apply a coat of pink polish over the entire nail. If you like a very natural finish, just apply one coat of pink polish; if you prefer a bolder effect, apply two coats.

4 Apply a clear top coat over the entire nail for added protection.

Pearly Polish

Even the shortest nails look great with a coat or two of polish that has a shimmering, pearlized finish. It's a soft, pretty look that suits everyone. Because it creates quite a subtle finish, you can wear it with any make-up look. Pearlized nail polish gives an especially pretty look in the summer and for holidays because the shiny particles glisten in the sunshine.

■ Pearly nail polish tends to give quite a sheer finish. Apply only one coat for a pretty, "barely there" effect.

■ Pearlized polish tends to chip more easily than other types, so be prepared to remove it after a couple of days. However, you can enhance its life by applying two coats of clear polish over the top to seal in the effect.

■ Originally, pearly polish was only available in a creamy mother-of-pearl finish, but today there are also purples, pinks and corals to choose from.

■ Some women with delicate skin find they're particularly sensitive to pearlized polish, so take care. Look for the hypo-allergenic variety.

Right: Build up the coats to intensify the finished result.

Right: Shimmering mother-of-pearl nails look good on everyone.

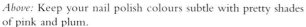
Above: Keep your nail polish colours subtle with pretty shades of pink and plum.

Above: Add a hint of shimmer to your nails.

Bright and Beautiful

Above: These days, coloured polishes break all the rules.

Below: Try painting a different colour on to each nail.

Nail polish colours have gone through a revolution recently. Now you're not just confined to reds and pinks. These days, you can buy a kaleidoscope of wild and wacky shades – from green to yellow, blue to silver. The choice is yours.

MAKING THE MOST OF BRIGHT COLOURS

■ Bright nail polish stains nails, so first apply at least one coat of clear base coat to prevent this from happening.

■ For fun, paint a different colour on to each nail – or alternate two colours.

■ Keep the rest of your make-up simple, or you'll end up with a really overpowering look!

■ If you're going to draw attention to your nails by using bright colours, they have to be in great condition. Indulge them with a weekly manicure.

■ Metallic finishes are very popular, but can be quite drying on the nails. Use a nourishing base coat underneath to prevent this, and go bare-nailed at least one day a week. If you do end up with stains on your nails, scrub them with a little facial scrub, then lightly buff the surface.

■ Even though they look dramatic in the bottle, some polishes look disappointingly sheer on the nail. You'll need to apply a few coats to build up the effect.

Right: Even if the rest of your make-up is subtle, your nails can be in striking colours.

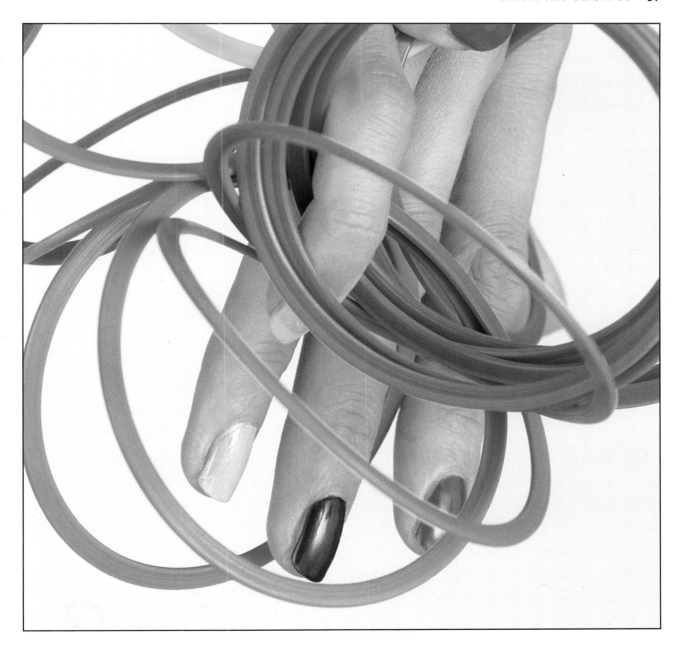

Get the Glitter Bug!

Once you've mastered some basic manicure techniques, have some fun and try some glittery looks.

■ Look out in stationery shops for larger glitter shapes, such as the stars used here (see far right). Pick up a single star shape with a pair of eyebrow tweezers and drop in place on a wet nail. Use the tip of the tweezer to ensure that it's secured. Again, apply a coat of clear polish to hold it in place for longer.

■ Some nail polishes have glitter already blended into them. The more coats you apply, the more glittery the finish will be.

■ A great way to add instant sparkle to ordinary nail polish is by sprinkling on a little loose glitter. Just sprinkle it over wet nail polish and leave to dry. Paint a clear coat of polish over the top to hold it in place for longer.

■ Another way to give your nails a pretty, speckled look is to apply a coat of bold colour and allow it to dry. Use a toothpick to dot a contrasting colour on the top.

Below: Liven up a clear polish with a sprinkling of glitter.

Above: These polishes come in a wide range of colours.

Right: Star spangled nails steal the show!

Fake It!

Artificial nails were first developed in Hollywood in the 1930s using basic plastics which were fine for photographic purposes but looked false in real life. Today's false nails are much more sophisticated, tougher and less likely to damage the nail underneath. There are four main types of false nails to choose from, depending on whether you want to replace a broken nail or have the instant gratification of a complete set of false nails.

Stick-on nails
These are precast plastic nail shapes that you apply with a special fixative or double-sided tape. They can be applied at home and look natural so long as you choose the right size. Most suppliers offer stick-on nails in a variety of nail widths.

Brush-on acrylic nails
The surface of the nail is first roughened and then the acrylic chemical is painted on and allowed to dry. It can then be styled into the desired shape. It grows out with your own nail. It is best carried out by a professional manicurist.

Nail extensions
These are made of plastic and are bonded to your nails with a special glue to ensure that they stay in place until your nail grows out. They can be filed as your nails get longer. Again, these are best applied by a professional manicurist.

Nail wrapping
This technique is used to reattach a broken nail tip to the nail or extend the length of your nails. A combination of fine tissue papers and fast drying glue is used to build up your nails. This is best left to a professional manicurist for good results.

Right: False nails can look as good as the real thing.

Below left: Take care to match the false stick-on nail to the shape of the nail bed.

Below: Nail wrapping is a technique which combines fine tissue papers and fast drying glue to build up your nails.

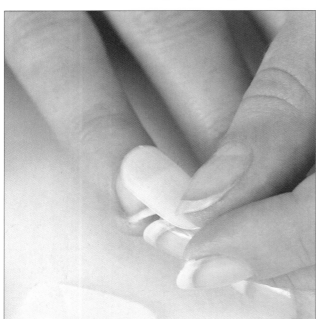

Protective Care for Summer Hands

Your hands need some extra special care when temperatures rise. The good news is, just a little special attention will ensure that they look their best at home or abroad.

Tip

Try storing your hand cream in the refrigerator. Not only will it keep the consistency firm, but chilled hand cream will make a refreshing treat for your hot hands during the summer months.

Above: Regular moisturizing with a sunscreen lotion or hand cream keeps the ageing effects of the sun at bay. Use all year round for maximum protection from the sun's ultraviolet rays.

THE SUNNY SIDE OF HANDCARE

■ Exposure to the sun is the main cause of skin ageing. In fact, experts believe that it's responsible for up to 90% of the visible signs of aging. Even if you're in your teens, it's essential to protect your hands from the ageing effects of the sun, because the damage you do now won't be evident for many years. Whatever your age, smooth the backs of your hands with a sunscreen lotion or a hand cream that filters out the sun's harmful ultraviolet rays. This will also help guard against the dangers of skin cancer – commonly found on the backs of hands because they face so much daily exposure.

■ Every night, apply a dot of nail strengthener oil to your nails, then apply your usual hand cream.

■ When you apply suntan lotion, rub a little into your nails. The oils will help counteract the drying effects of the sun.

■ Before starting to do gardening, first scrape your nails over a bar of soap or soapy nail brush. The undersides of your nails will fill up with soap, acting as a barrier against dirt, grime and infection.

■ Holidays are the perfect time to experiment with new polish colours. Tropical colours and pearly whites look great against lightly tanned fingers.

Right: Hot weather tactics make for beautiful nails.

Below: Try scraping your nails over soap or a soapy nail brush before gardening.

Soothing Care for Winter Hands

Freezing temperatures, biting winds and central heating can literally strip the skin on your hands of their natural oils. It can also weaken your nails, leaving them dry and flaky. Just as you need to lavish extra care on your face and body at this time of year, the same applies to your hands.

ICE MAIDEN TACTICS

The low concentration of oil glands in the back of your hands means that this area lacks natural protection. In winter, frequent washing and contact with detergents makes them even more vulnerable than your face. Choose a hand cream that contains a high level of protection and apply by massaging it into your hands first, then working up to your wrists. Just as your skin needs a richer moisturizer at this time of year, your hands may also need a more nourishing hand cream, so switch from runny liquids to thick creams. Thicker creams also have a higher oil content that will help seal extra moisture into the upper layers of your skin.

■ Take extra care to dry your hands thoroughly after washing. Any remaining dampness on the skin will freeze in the cold air, leading to soreness and chapping.

■ Treat your hands to a hand mask. You can either use a moisturizing face mask or improvise with a rich hand cream. Simply smooth over your hands, working the cream right down to the tips of your nails. Leave to soak into your skin for 10-20 minutes. Then wipe off the excess and rub in any residue.

■ Protect your hands from the outside elements by investing in warm gloves.

■ If you have weak nails, use a cotton-bud (swab) with a pointed end to clean under the free edge — it's gentler than scrubbing with a nail brush.

Right: Beautiful hands — even when temperatures fall below zero.

Below left: Lavish your hands with the same care as you give your complexion and you will soon reap the benefits!

Below: Switch to a richer cream to increase your skin's moisture levels.

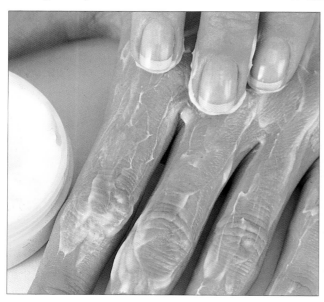

How to Beat the Nail Biting Habit

The most expensive manicure in the world will be worthless if you bite your nails. It's a very hard habit to break, but one worth beating if you're serious about having beautiful hands and nails.

TIPS TO STOP NAIL BITING

■ Devote 10 minutes a day to caring for your nails. As your nails look a bit better, you'll be more inclined to stick with it.

■ Try one of the anti-bite lotions that are on the market. Once you've stopped for a couple of weeks, your longer nails will give you the incentive to keep up the good work.

■ If you have short nails, it doesn't mean you shouldn't use nail polish. Even the stubbiest, shortest nails look better for an application of clear or pale pearly polish.

■ Consider wearing false nails for a while so your nails have a chance to grow underneath. Even the most determined of nail biters have trouble gnawing through them! Just a few weeks is often all it takes to break the habit.

■ Some former nail biters say that restricting themselves to just one nail can do the trick. Once you see how nice the other nails look, you'll be inspired to grow out the bitten one.

■ If you bite your nails because you're feeling stressed or nervous, try playing with a set of worry beads instead.

■ Use scented hand cream – the taste of the perfume will put you off biting!

> **Tip**
> Carry a nail file with you at all times. That way you can instantly smooth away straggly edges that will tempt you to bite.

Right: Break the biting habit for beautiful nails.

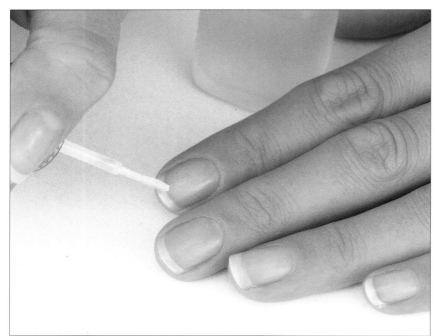

Above: Invest in an anti-bite lotion. Just one nibble could put you off the biting habit for life!

Left: Apply the anti-bite lotion every day to ensure success.

20 Quick Tips for Beautiful Hands

It's often the small things that make all the difference to the way your nails look.

1 Pay for your manicure beforehand – rummaging for cash can ruin fresh polish.
2 Dunk freshly polished nails into a bowl of iced water to help polish dry quickly.
3 To extend the life of your polish, clean the top of the bottle with a tissue after applying – polish buildup allows air into the bottle and the product evaporates.
4 Cheap nail polishes thicken with age – dilute them with a base coat to make them last longer.
5 Prolong the life of your manicure by painting on a top coat every other day.

6 Make a polish last longer by washing your nails in warm soapy water. Then wipe your nails thoroughly with a tissue to remove any residues before applying a layer of polish.
7 Ink or nicotine stains can be bleached away by rubbing your fingers with a slice of neat lemon. Rub in lots of hand cream afterwards to counteract the drying effects.
8 Dry nails quickly by blasting gently with the cool air flow button of your hair dryer.
9 Store nail polishes in the refrigerator to prevent them from becoming too thick – it helps prevent evaporation and the polish stays liquid for longer.

10 Rub a little petroleum jelly around the neck of a new bottle of polish to prevent it from sticking in future.
11 When removing nail polish, swish the cotton wool (cotton balls) from the base of your nail to the tip so you don't have to push drying nail polish remover into your delicate cuticles.
12 Don't just use the tip of the brush when applying polish or you'll risk applying too much polish. The brush should be splayed out against the nail horizontally. This means you'll get thinner, more even layers of polish – which means a more professional finish.
13 Don't apply polish in the sunshine – the polish will bubble as it dries.

Above: Lather up before a manicure to ensure streak-free nails.

Right: A base coat over and under the nail will help to strengthen it.

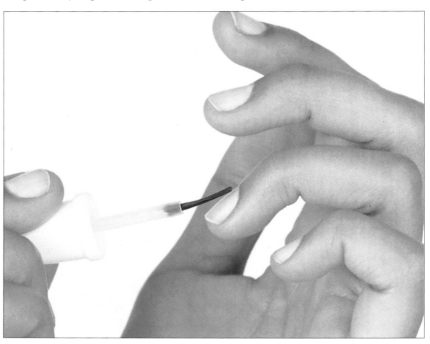

14 If you mess up a nail and you're pressed for time, you don't have to take off all the polish. Instead, dampen the pad of your opposite index finger with nail polish remover and pat over the messy nail. The globby polish will smooth out sufficiently so you can let it dry and apply polish over it.

15 Apply a mud face pack to the backs of your hands for deep-down cleansing. Apply lots of nourishing hand cream afterwards.

16 Remove any traces of polish on surrounding skin with a cottonbud (swab) dipped in nail polish remover.

17 For the illusion of longer, slimmer nails, leave a very slight space at either side of the nail when painting.

18 If you've run out of polish remover, try this tip: coat your nail with some clear base coat. Let it set for 45 seconds, then press cotton wool (cotton balls) over the nail and remove – the base coat and colour will come off in one fell swoop.

19 Paint your base coat up and around the tip of the nail to strengthen your nails and help prevent breakages.

20 A pumice stone is not just for feet! Using one gently on your hands is a good way to remove ingrained dirt and stains.

Below left: Sweep off polish from base to tip to protect your cuticles.

Below: A top coat will keep nails looking good every day.

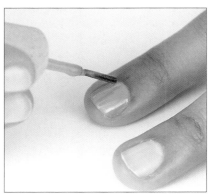

Above: Apply polish thinly. Several thin coats of polish give a more professional finish than one or two thick layers.

Manicure Q&A

Whatever your nailcare problems, we've got the answers!

Q: "The tips of my nails look discoloured. What can I do about them?"
A: Dip a cottonbud (swab) in some neat lemon juice and work it under the nail. Leave for 10 minutes. Rinse well afterwards and apply lots of hand cream to counteract the drying effects.

Q: "I've noticed that some nail polishes are labelled as hypo-allergenic and suitable for sensitive skins. Surely your nails can't be allergic to nail polish?"
A: Your nails aren't but your skin can be! Remember that we constantly touch our faces with our hands throughout the day. If you're sensitive to the ingredients in nail polish, you may set up a reaction – such as red, inflamed skin around your eyes, lips and nose. However, hypo-allergenic nail polish is less likely to set off an irritation because the ingredients that are likely to cause it have been removed.

Q: "Costume jewellery causes an allergic reaction on my fingers. Is there anything I can do, without having to throw it out?"
A: Coat the inside of the jewellery with some hypo-allergenic clear nail polish. Also, make sure you're not building up a residue of soap under your rings, which can irritate the skin.

Q: "Is there anything I can do to get rid of ridges on my nails?"
A: Most nails have ridges in the surface, running from the cuticle to the tip. If they're quite prominent, you can gently buff the surface of your nail with a nail buffer to make them less obvious. However, go gently and take care not to

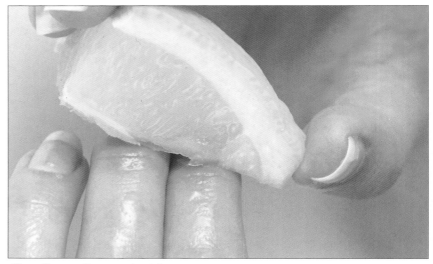

Above: Say goodbye to stained fingers with a slice of lemon. Rub the lemon juice and rind over the stained area.

thin the nails. Most nailcare companies also offer a product called a ridge filler, which you apply under your nail polish to fill in the ridges and create a smoother surface on which to work.

Q: "Why does a nail turn black if it's been damaged?"
A: If you trap your finger in a door, it will turn black because the nail bed bleeds. The blood has nowhere to go, so dries and attaches itself to the nail bed. You can lessen the effects by dunking your damaged finger in ice cold water to help stop the bleeding.

Q: "Is there anything I can do to get rid of nicotine or ink stains on my fingers?"
A: Rub half a lemon (both juice and rind) over the affected area. If stains are persistent, try lightly buffing with a nail buffer.

Above: Applying toothpaste with a brush helps to remove nicotine or ink stains.

Alternatively, try applying a touch of toothpaste with a brush.

Right: The French manicure looks good with everything.

Foot Notes

Anyone can have pretty feet if they give them some attention. But the truth of the matter is, most of us ignore our feet until we want to wear revealing shoes or open-toe sandals. However, feet respond best to a little care every day rather than a major blitz every once in a while. So, kick off your shoes and give your feet the pampering they deserve!

PLAYING FOOTSIE

This is the essential kit you need to ensure that your feet get the TLC they deserve:

Nail clippers

Using nail clippers is the best way to cut the thick nails on your feet without causing any splitting.

Emery board

This is used to smooth away any hard edges after clipping your toenails. Look for longer ones, as it'll be easier to reach your toes.

Toe separators

These allow you to apply polish to your nails without smudging it on to your toes.

Pumice stone

This is used to gently rub away patches of hard skin from the soles and sides of your feet.

Foot lotion

Apply this every day to keep the skin on your feet soft and smooth, and to help avoid a buildup of hard skin.

Cuticle cream

Rub over the cuticles of your toenails once a week to soften them and make them easier to push back.

Hoof stick

The rubber tip of a hoof stick helps you to gently push cuticles back after applying cuticle cream.

Clear polish

Just one coat of clear, shiny colour on your toenails will make your feet look better.

Polish remover

Use to remove old polish before applying a new coat.

DID YOU KNOW?

■ There are 26 bones and 115 ligaments in each foot, as well as tendons and muscles, all of which are arranged to create several dynamic arches that support the body weight.

■ On average, we take 18,000 steps a day.

■ Each time our feet hit the floor, double the weight of our body impacts with the floor.

■ Over 50% of women don't like their feet, probably as a result of foot problems. The good news is that you can do things to make your feet look more attractive.

■ Our feet contain around 250,000 sweat glands and they perspire more than any other part of our body. On average, each foot produces an eggcupful (a 1/2 cup) of sweat each day.

■ In our lifetime, it's estimated that our feet carry us an average of 70,000 miles (112,000 km) – or almost three times around the world.

■ The average foot size has increased over the past 100 years from size 3 (5 USA) to size 6 (8 USA).

Left: Everything you need for pretty feet. Clockwise from bottom left: pumice stone; clippers; hoof stick; emery board; foot lotion; polish remover; clear polish; cuticle cream; toe separators.

Right: Feet respond best to a little care every day – regular care makes feet fit to flaunt.

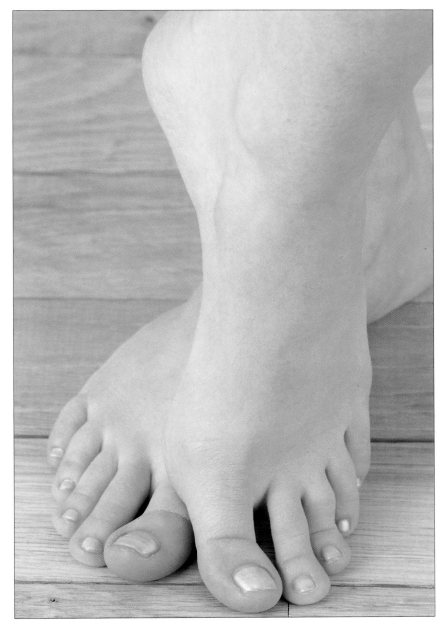

Easy Steps to Softer Feet

Considering the punishment they take, it's no wonder that feet develop areas of hard skin and callouses. These tips will help keep the skin soft, supple and smooth.

■ Soak your feet in a bowl of warm soapy water to soften hard skin.

■ To really soften areas of rough skin, add 30ml/2 tbsp of bicarbonate of soda (baking soda) to the warm water. Soak your feet for 15 minutes before setting to work with a pumice stone.

■ Smooth away problem areas with a foot file or pumice stone. Work over the heels, sides and soles of your feet, but leave the toes well alone.

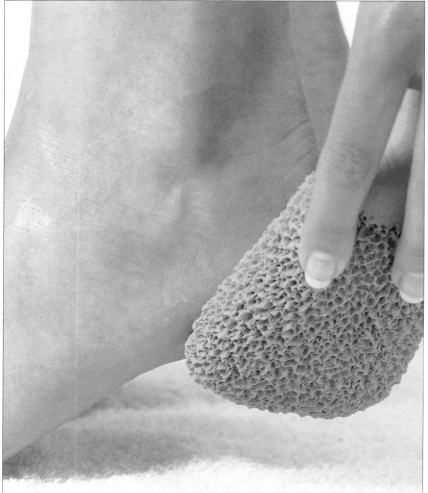

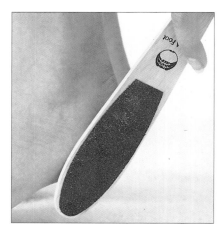

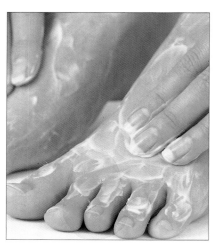

■ If you don't have a pumice stone, use an ordinary body scrub instead.

■ The secret of dealing with hard skin is to gently rub it away every day rather than trying to remove it in one session. Otherwise, you'll risk ending up with red, sore feet.

■ Apply foot cream to your feet every day, rubbing it in well and avoiding the spaces between the toes. Take the time to knead and massage every inch of the sole, heel and top side of the foot.

■ If you have a big buildup of hard skin, you should see a qualified chiropodist rather than trying to remove it yourself.

■ Once a week, rub your feet with a thick layer of cream, pull on a pair of socks and head for bed. Your feet will be much softer in the morning.

Far left: Use a pumice stone, a foot scrub or a foot file to remove any hard skin and keep your feet healthy. Concentrate on the parts of your feet where hard skin builds up – especially the heels.

Top left: A foot file is another alternative to a pumice stone.

Left: Treat your feet to a regular relaxing massage.

Right: A foot bath provides a soothing heat – and an effective cure for hard skin, too.

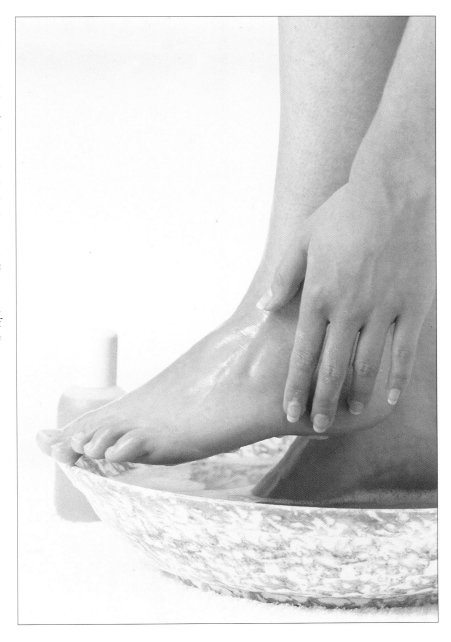

The Quick and Easy Pedicure

This weekly pedicure will ensure that your toenails always look presentable.

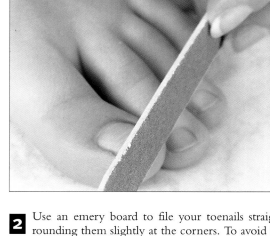

1 Cut off any excess toenail with a pair of nail clippers, working straight across the nail. Avoid using nail scissors as these can split the nail and cause ingrowing toenails.

2 Use an emery board to file your toenails straight across, rounding them slightly at the corners. To avoid ingrowing toenails, don't file into the corners of the nails. Hold the board slightly angled down towards the free edge of the nail and smooth from each side of the nail towards the centre.

3 Massage a little cuticle cream into the base of your nails.

4 Push back your cuticle with a hoof stick or a cottonbud (swab). Use circular movements for greatest effect. Wipe off any excess cream, and finish with a coat of clear nail polish.

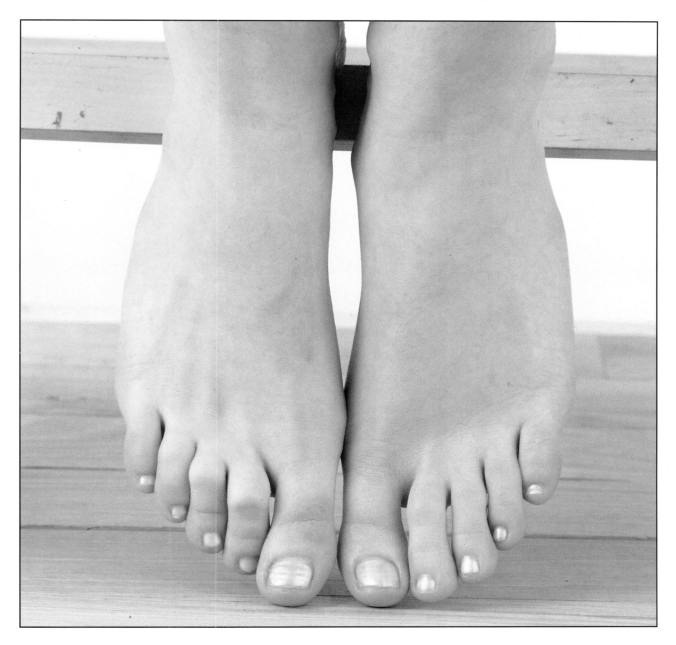

Fancy Footwork

If you love bright-coloured nail polishes but find they're too overpowering on your fingernails, then try wearing them on your toes! A flash of bright colour under sandals or mules will instantly brighten up a summer or evening look.

TIPS FOR PAINTED TOENAILS

■ If your feet and toes aren't your best feature, it's a good idea to try a clear, pearlized or pale-coloured nail polish so you don't draw too much attention to them.

■ Because your feet have to be pushed into shoes, polish often gets smudged on your toenails. Even if the polish is dry to the touch, it's still liable to be wet for a few hours after application. It's best to paint your toenails when you know you won't need to wear shoes for a while.

Right: Sponge toe separators stop your polish smudging.

Far right: If your feet look good, show them off with bright polish.

Above: Before you apply nail polish, try separating your toes either with a foam rubber separator, by using cotton wool (cotton balls), or twist a tissue into a narrow strip and weave it in and out of your toes to prevent smudging. Apply a clear base coat to create a smooth surface on which to work and to prevent bright nail polishes from staining your toenails. Then apply two coats of coloured nail polish.

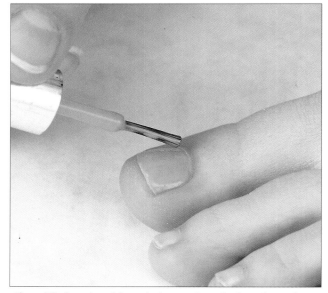

Above: Work each nail by painting a stripe of colour down the centre, and then overlapping with a strip of colour down each side. Leave each coat to dry thoroughly. Apply a clear top coat to seal in the colour and make it extra hardwearing. Leave it to dry as long as you can before putting on your shoes. At least an hour is recommended as even socks and tights can leave their imprints if put on too soon.

Pedicure Q&A

We've got the answers to your foot-care problems!

Q: "How can I be sure I'm choosing the right size shoes?"
A: Try these tips:
■ Feel your foot through the leather to ensure a comfortable fit. Bulges can be a sign that there is pressure on a toe.

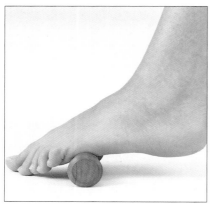

Above: Try rolling your feet over a foot massager after a long, hard day.

■ Take a short walk wearing the shoe and check for slipping or gaping.
■ Never buy shoes you know are too small in the hope they'll stretch – they'll definitely damage your feet.
■ Buy shoes in the late afternoon when your feet are at their largest.
■ If your feet tend to swell in summer, try sandals on when your feet are swollen or buy half a size larger.
■ Shoes should have good support under the heel and instep and have enough room for the feet to spread inside the shoes.

■ High heels throw the body's alignment off balance, so wear them as little as possible. Choose shoes with a low heel and a flexible sole to allow the ligaments and muscles of the sole to be exercised.
Q: "Is there anything I can do to perk my feet up at the end of a hard day?"
A: Any of these tips will help:
■ Lie down with your feet higher than your head for 10 minutes.
■ Roll your feet over a foot massager. It will improve the circulation in your feet.
■ Massage your feet with a tingling mint foot gel.
■ Give your feet a friction rub with a towel, then massage them with cologne – it'll feel wonderful as it evaporates.
■ Sit on the edge of the bath with your feet under the tap at full pressure. Start with warm water, increase to hot, then gradually turn to cold. Stay there for as long as you can, then dry your feet.

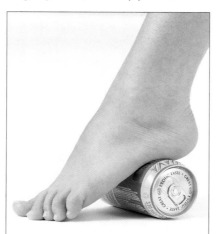

Above: Roll your feet over a can of cold drink straight from the refrigerator!

Q: "How can I make sure my trainers (sneakers) give my feet the protection they need?"
A: Check that they fulfil these conditions:
■ They should be lightweight with adequate cushioning to absorb impact on landing and reduce stress on the joints.
■ They should support your feet to help prevent twists and strains. The kind of shoe you choose depends on the exercise you're doing. For instance, aerobics shoes have extra support in the arches and on the outside. It's worth buying a pair of cross trainers (sneakers) if you do several different types of activities. Whatever you do, buy your shoes at a good sports store where the staff can advise you on the best shoe for your needs.
■ Take your last pair of trainers (sneakers) with you, so the shop assistant can see which part of the shoe you wear down the most and then advise you properly.

Right: Perfect care for pretty feet.

Below: Spritz your feet with a deodorizing foot spray before putting on your shoes in the morning.

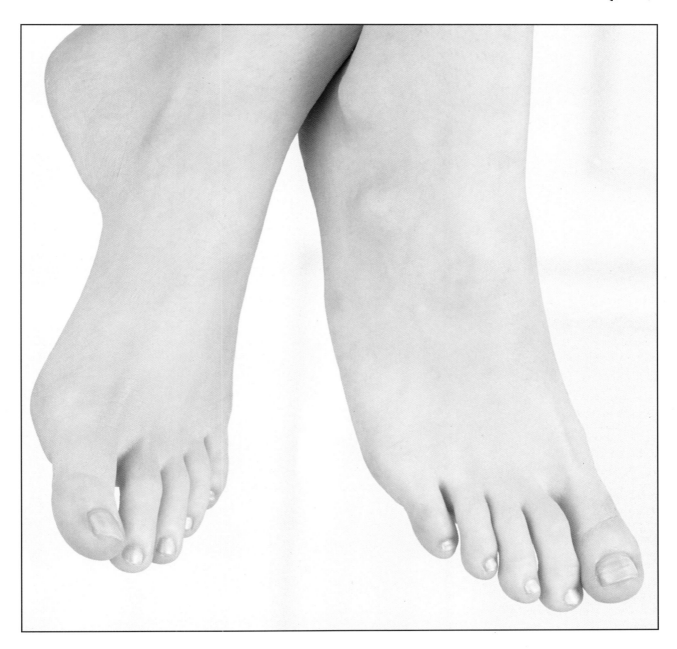

Manicure and Pedicure Buzzwords

This is a brief A to Z of manicure and pedicure words. If you're not sure what it means, look it up here:

Athlete's foot
A highly contagious fungal infection that thrives in damp warm areas of the skin, especially between the toes. The skin splits and is accompanied by an itchy rash. There are good treatments that you can buy at the chemist, but consult your doctor if the condition doesn't clear up. To avoid it in the first place, wear flip flops in communal changing rooms, don't share towels and keep feet clean and dry between washes.

Bunion
An enlargement of the toe joint, usually on the big toe. It's usually caused by shoes that are too tight and is often very painful.

Calluses
General patches of hard skin on the feet caused by an uneven displacement of

Below: Use a pumice stone every day.

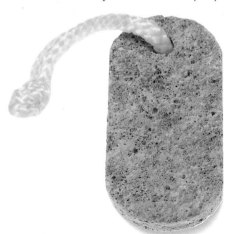

body weight. Guard against them by wearing comfortable shoes and using a pumice stone to rub away dry spots of skin as they appear.

Corns
Usually found on the toes, corns develop as a result of pressure or friction. You can buy corn pads at the chemist; but see a qualified chiropodist if they don't clear up.

Cuticle
The thin strip of skin that protects the living cells under your nail from any possible infection.

Hangnails
Pieces of skin torn away from but still attached to the base or side of a fingernail. They're usually caused when the cuticles have dried and cracked.

Hoof stick
A manicure stick with a rubber tip used to push back your cuticles.

Ingrowing toenail
Incorrect trimming and filing of the nails can cause the edge to grow into the skin. These are usually very painful and should be treated by a doctor or chiropodist. Don't be tempted to ease or cut the nail yourself or you'll risk infection.

Keratin
A protein substance that forms the base of your nails.

Lunula
Also known as the "half moon" at the base of your nails.

Leuconychia
These white spots are either caused by general wear and tear or by blows to the matrix of the nail. They grow out naturally with the nail.

Matrix
The area just beneath the cuticle where new nail cells are formed. It's the actively growing tissue.

Nail plate
The visible part of the nail that rests on the nail bed.

Verruca
A highly contagious viral wart-like infection found on the sole of the foot. The surface of the skin appears rough or granular, often with small black dots in the centre. You can usually get rid of them by using remedies from the chemist. If they persist, have them checked or removed by your doctor.

Right: Hands and feet to be proud of.

Below: Scrub up your act.

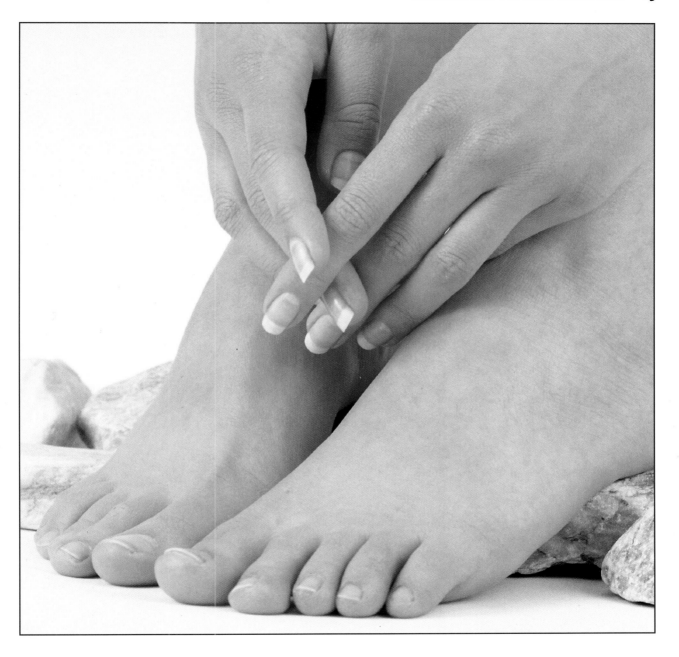

Index

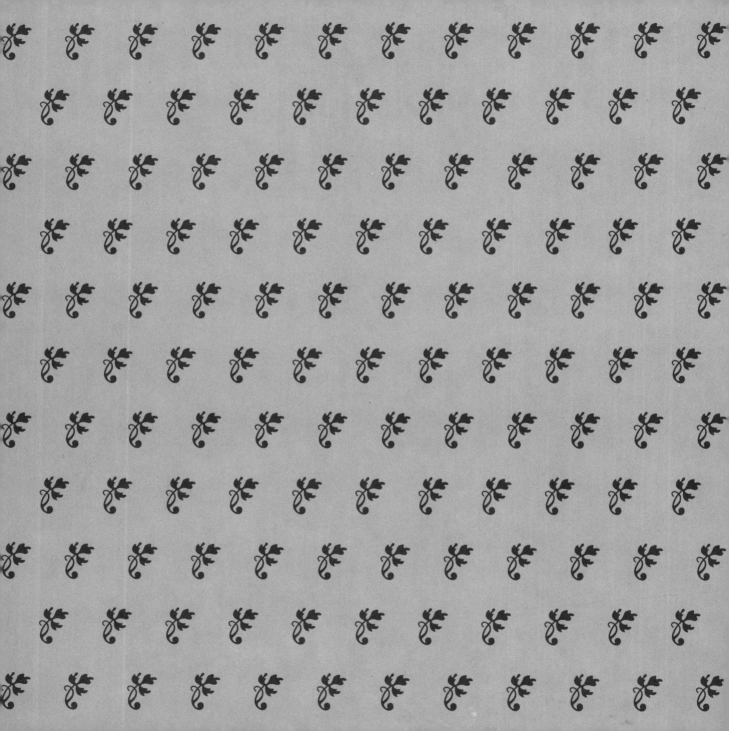